T0207687

FIRM, FAIR
AND
CONSISTENT

FOUNDATIONAL TERMINOLOGY FOR SUCCESSFUL LIVING

TS BOLA

authorHOUSE®

AuthorHouse™
1663 Liberty Drive
Bloomington, IN 47403
www.authorhouse.com
Phone: 1 (800) 839-8640

Published by AuthorHouse 11/05/2019

ISBN: 978-1-7283-3498-1 (sc)
ISBN: 978-1-7283-3496-7 (hc)
ISBN: 978-1-7283-3497-4 (e)

Library of Congress Control Number: 2019918016

Print information available on the last page.

BOOK DEDICATION

This book writing is dedicated to my wonderful high school
teachers and especially to Mrs. Lilly
Robinson, my English teacher.
Her influence caused me to develop an
academic preference for grammar
and vocabulary, which facilitated the
writing abilities that I may have.
Additionally, I want to recognize and
thank my brother Terry for his very
persistent urging for me to write this
book, based on the three words he
appreciated so much, "Firm, Fair and Consistent."
I thank you all very much, for I could not
have done this without your support.

PREFACE

Greetings to all of you readers of this book! I am writing this Preface in a very personal manner, as if we were sitting in your living room and possibly discussing various applications from this system of "Firm, Fair and Consistent" (FFC). As such, I certainly hope that this type of presentation does not disturb too much, your concept of how, or in what manner, a published book should be presented. I must confess that after many years of writing psychological reports in a rather formal manner, I have decided to write in a more relaxed and personal manner, in the presenting of the information that I am inspired to present here.

In order to adjust your perspective just a small amount, I wish to give you a review of my personal background, as it is said, so you can "know from where I am coming." I hope that you will possibly better understand, from my type of background presentation, how and why I have arrived at believing and expressing the concepts and perspectives, which

I present in this publication. As such, let us go to the mini-biography as I have indicated. And by the way, quotes from the Bible that I give here, come from the Recovery Version (2003).

At this writing, I have entered my 81st year and will likely have my 82nd birthday party before this book is published. In my opinion, this alone speaks volumes, in reference to social/spiritual experiences that I have had, and surely, in reference to seeing the many changes in our USA social system over those many years since the "Great Depression." I was born in 1937, living most of my life in a small Texas town and having most of my education there, including high school. We were a family of very modest means. I am the eldest of six children in my family (three males and three females), with the age span of over sixteen years.

Now, two of my siblings have passed away, leaving two males and two females. My parents and we the children are Christian believers. My mother was a Southern Baptist church member all her life and we all attended Sunday church meetings. As such, you could say that we had a fairly strict lower-middleclass upbringing. My Dad was a hard-working oilfield-type worker, for T&P Coal & Oil Co. And when I was in college, I was allowed to work with the same company, during summer break. Both Dad and Mom were fairly strict disciplinarians and for sure, we learned quite quickly, that we had best not "cross or challenge" my Dad's principles, words, or guidelines. Otherwise, we would be facing immediate chastisement, usually of a physical punishment nature. He was very "hard" on me as the eldest one; I guess, as an example to the others. He had a "quick temper" and it took very little to ignite it!

I always wondered why he had such a quick temper, but later I imagined the reason for that was; he had an abusive father who roughly treated his children and even his wife. For this reason my father left home in Louisiana, at 14 years of age and came to work in the East Texas oilfield. But several years later he decided to gravitate over more to the west, where the "oil boom" had started in 1917, with the discovery of the McClesky Oilwell #1. Then later on, after Dad had married and divorced his first wife and married my mother, I was born in 1937 and lived in that area for most of my young life, except for the 5 years that we lived farther out in West Texas, when my Dad was transferred there to the Permian Basin Oilfield.

In my growing-up I enjoyed very much the sport of football and I played it many years. As a matter of fact, that was the main reason that I wanted to attend high school and not for the academics. As such, I just barely graduated from my high school, mainly because all I wanted to do was to play football. But anyway, I made enough passing grades so I would be eligible to play football. However, my practice was not all in vain, because we had a good enough team in 1953 to win the Class A, Texas State Championship. Well, thank God, I was so dedicated to football; not that I was a great talent, but because it required a certain discipline. This was good for me, because I was a very active and aggressive boy growing-up and my adhering to the sport's discipline and regimen was good for training and controlling me.

Yes, I know what you are likely thinking. Probably something like, "How could this dumb football player write a book and even get it published?" I do not think negatively of you, if you would think that way, because the evidence that is given here might suggest that concept. Well, just to set the record straight, I not only have written this book, but it is my third book to publish. As such, maybe soon I will be known as an "author." However, remember this old adage, "Don't judge the book by its cover," or <u>pre-judge</u> one's native potential or ability. At that time in my life, I just was not at the stage, or "readiness point," to value academic lessons, for gaining academic knowledge. But thank God, He made some needed adjustments in me.

However, the "readiness factor" did arrive within me a few years later. Otherwise, I would not be writing this now. As it happened, my favorite teacher, one whom I now remember as being a very dedicated teacher, was Mrs. Lilly Robinson, my English teacher. By some means, she inspired me to develop some interest in vocabulary and grammar. That may sound peculiar, especially coming from an apparently "simple minded athlete," but it has helped me tremendously over the years in conversing, writing my psychological reports, writing poetry and as you can see, writing my third book. Then, after I graduated from high school, I attended two years of junior college. I also served three years in the National Guard.

Next, after having worked in the oilfields for a while, I joined the US Army and spent over three years in the US Army, two of which were served in Munich, Germany. I was there when the Russians put-up the so-called "Berlin Wall" and we were on alert 24/7 for quite a while. Anyway, while there, I studied and even became semi-fluent in the German language. However later, after my living more than fifty years in West Texas, with practically no one with whom to speak German, I have lost the speaking function of German. Fortunately, after my return to the USA, marrying, having children (Brian, 57, and later, Jason, 50, & Katherine, 48) and working in the West Texas oilfield again, I returned to study in a Texas college.

I changed my college major from Geology to Physical & Health Education & Spanish. I would guess that the extreme change of academic emphasis was due to my lifetime liking of football. So, after graduation, I started coaching three sports and teaching Spanish and Physical Education in a public school system in the state of New Mexico. I did that until I became very interested in the subject of human motivation, which pointed me in the direction of starting to study the profession of Psychology, in the courses of my Master Degree (MEd).

After getting my Master Degree and studying Psychology and Counseling for two more post-graduate degrees, (Educational Specialist, EdS and a PhD in Psychology), I started to work in public schools as a Psychologist, teaching Spanish and Special Education. As I reflect back on those years of much studying and education, while working and being married with children, and earning those four degrees, I really do not know how I had that much energy to complete all of that! All I can say is that, the Good Lord just took good care of me and the family.

I also was working in private practice doing my specialty of Psychometrics; that is, doing Psychological evaluations for physicians, Juvenile Probation and also various Sheriff's departments. I also learned that in West Texas, one who is "bilingual" in Spanish and English, has an advantage over others who are not, for getting jobs that serve the general public. Additionally, I worked as the Clinical Supervisor in a Juvenile Prison in this state of Texas, for eight years. After that kind of experience, counseling and evaluating deviant juveniles, my opinion is that you probably could not tell me a story, or some sort of fabrication, that I have not heard! I observed that juvenile delinquents are quite "creative" in their stories.

Those were tough experiences, but they were very helpful for me in my profession. Also, mixed-in with all those educational, professional, social and vocational situations, unfortunately, I experienced matrimonial divorce. But even though I lamented over that, I finally encountered the love of my life, Socorro, of Durango, Mexico. By the way, her name, Socorro in Spanish, translates in English "timely help." And she has been quite timely and also helpful for me, in more than thirty years of a good marriage. She has been what I could say, as a "cap," on my many experiences and is extremely part of me, as my true counterpart!

I must also say that now that I am somewhat into my "twilight" years, she surely does look after me, to take care of my health and dietary needs and occasionally, she even encourages me in what I do! She does all that care-taking, as well as, having acquired her Master Degree in Bilingual Education, teaches elementary school and has done most of the work in helping raise-up two wonderful children (Ana, 35 & Tomás, 33), as well as an adopted son from Mexico, (Luis Carlos, 39). They are now grown and also are college-educated. So, may the Good Lord reward her for being so patient and caring with me over these many years! The Good Lord and my family are the "main-stays" in my life!!

This synopsis should "set the scene," so you may understand "from where I am coming." Maybe you will see and even agree, to some extent, that FFC truly should be applied to all our living situations as we pass through this world. I hope that you will enjoy this presentation and that the information contained in this book will be useful to you now or, if not now, at least some time in your future journey on this Earth.

CONTENTS

Chapter One

THE FACTUAL CONCEPTS OF FIRM, FAIR AND CONSISTENT

FIRST, IT IS BEST TO give a clear definition for the meaning of the term, FIRM, as the first term used in this tripartite concept. As such, let us go to the Random House dictionary. This is their definition in summary: "not soft or yielding when pressed; comparatively solid, hard; securely fixed in place; steady and not shaky or trembling; not likely to change, settled; un-alterable; steadfast, unwavering, as persons or principles; indicating determination." A second definition is also given, which is a derivative of the same Latin root word: "firmament," meaning, "the vault of heaven or sky." Both definitions are based on the Latin word, *firmare*, meaning, "to strengthen or to confirm." Yes, I know that this may sound like teaching in grade school class. However, this clarification is always important in order to have adequate communication and have a clear understanding of the terminology that we are using. That way, both of us will be on the "same page," as the saying goes. Defining this word gives a strong base from which to explain how it is used in the basic tripartite function of managing personal, social, family, spiritual and/or vocational/business issues.

Second, I wish to give a "fair" definition of the word, FAIR, using the same dictionary. This is their definition in summary: "free from bias, dishonesty or injustice; legitimately sought, pursued, done or given; proper under the rules; marked by favoring conditions; likely promising for success; unobstructed; not blocked-up; free from blemish, imperfection, or anything that impairs the quality, appearance or character; honest, just, straightforward; unbiased, equitable." As such, the word "fair" comes from old German, *fagar*, which is related to the word "clear." Certainly, in our dealings with others, being fair in a relationship is also being "clear," as to what our intentions are and what we expect from the course of the relationship. Yes, it should be understood that most young children within our caretaking relationship will not likely understand what our intentions are for them in their guiding and training process. However, in dealing with older children and adults it is very good to express ourselves in a fair and clear manner, so there are no misunderstandings between us, or least very few.

Understanding this word usage is another step forward into the utilization of the tripartite process of this management system. However, the word "fair" brings up a variety of mental images and expectations in various people. And as such, the useful application of the "fair" concept will certainly need to be carefully used in accordance to the formal and moral rules and guidelines within your work environment, society, home and/or your spiritual realm. In this manner, people can basically have a "clear conscience" in their dealings with others, including the upbringing of their own children. This is a personal type advantage for the use of this "fair" relationship management process, in dealing with the <u>self</u> and others.

Now thirdly, we come to the last of this tripartite composition, which is CONSISTENT. Using the same dictionary, their definition is short, indicating: "not self-contradictory; constantly adhering to the same principles, course, form, etc.; holding firmly together; cohering, firm, solid, retaining form." This word comes from the Latin base word of, *consistere*, which basically means, congruous and/or consonant. As such, we probably can see and understand how important this word is for us, as we put into practice its meaning and concept in relationships. I would ask you this question: Have you ever had a relationship with someone who behaved in an inconsistent manner, in one or more situations, especially in which you had to depend on his appropriate action? I am quite sure that you remember the frustration and even anger that you experienced from that situation. As such, I am also quite sure we can see and understand the necessity for "consistency" in relationships. This is especially true where one or more people (including your children) are there expecting and depending on us or someone to be responsible and dependable in supplying, giving, and/or doing something, or as we are saying here, to be consistent in what is expected in the given situation.

Being consistent in performing our job requirements, or our family obligations, or doing homework lesson assignments, or being on time for meetings and quite a multitude of other situations, is necessary. That is, it is necessary if we intend to maintain a reasonably positive relationship in the various scenarios in which we involve ourselves on a daily basis. Therefore, positive consistency is likely one of the most important characteristics that we can develop, in order that we can have any hope of having a successful vocational career, family and personal life. Notice, I have emphasized the phrase "positive consistency" in this presentation. I believe that you know some people with negative attitudes and behaviors, who continue "consistently" to do the same thing, over and over, while expecting a positive change. This erroneous behavior is pure lunacy.

An example of this is like drug addicts, continually abusing cocaine or heroin. They seek and have a short moment of "ecstasy," but later crave more and more and are not able to function well "normally" in a vocation, in society, or in a family situation, and also are in conflict with the law. Some would say, "Oh, but these types of people are addicted and cannot control their poor behavior anymore." And I would reply that, "Even addicts and/or sick persons know that they need help." I believe that most of us would look at their situation and think, that with so much failure in their living situation, they should be convinced to stop their <u>negative consistency</u> and start seeking a wholesome lifestyle. Or, if they are not strong enough to do it alone, then get help to do it. When these types of people are on the "down side" and experiencing discomfort and pain, it is sad that they do not seek a positive resolution. Yes, I know that there are a few of them who have become "recovered addicts." And most of those who did it were those who decided that they had suffered enough pain and so, finally they decided to make a change. Remember the old saying once again, "Stupidity (and insanity) is doing the same thing, time after time and expecting a different result." I cannot answer for you, but I certainly do not want to be one included in that scenario!

As an ex-football coach, I must say that I have seen similar results in action with some teams who were losers. I have also seen winners, who when their playing strategies were not appearing to work well, they immediately changed their game plan in order to adjust to the demands of the given situation. Practically every time this happened there was, at least, some degree of success in progress. As such, in our <u>positive consistency</u>, we need to be observant and know when to consistently change our usual "consistent" way of functioning; that is, if we see the situation warrants it. This may sound a bit like "inconsistent," but if you will sharply consider it, you will see that it makes perfectly good sense to do so. It is referred to as, "adjusting to the demands of the situation at hand." That is, this tactic makes good sense, if you wish to have a good opportunity of having a successful relationship, or a successful endeavor. I believe that a good example was given of this "adjusting concept," in the Post Script section at the end of this book. It involved a man making a vocational adjustment from the very late 19th Century and then, entering the early 20th Century. As such, one should take caution and be watchful for "needed" adjustments in the various living areas of family, education, vocation, society and spiritual needs.

Chapter Two

MARITAL AND FAMILY APPLICATIONS

FROM THE BEGINNING OF ONE'S marital aspirations, in seeking a spouse, it is likely that the search for a spouse would include the idea of expecting the spouse to be a fair-minded person and consistently so. Now, in reference to firmness, one may not think very much about that concept, at least until a situation would arise that reveals that aspect in a positive or negative manner. One who seeks a spouse and is oriented within the scope of this presentation, of my true tripartite management philosophy, will be "present-minded" about the concept and usage of "Firm, Fair and Consistent" (FFC), for daily living. Otherwise, other people will likely have a "hit-or-miss" condition of personal knowledge, in reference to this process. As such, the first mentioned seeker of a spouse will be conscious of the specific characteristics sought after in a spouse. On the other hand, the second one would likely only be partially alert to this concept and mainly make a decision based on physical appearance, feelings and/or emotional aspects of the person. It is best to have an "overall" perception, in choosing a spouse.

When one considers the true importance of those three words in this tripartite management process, along with other positive characteristics, it is easy to understand how couples have success or failure in marriages. In this country of the United States of America it appears quite obvious that with around 50% of marriages here ending in divorce, there is definitely something very important that is missing in the marriages. Otherwise, there would be a greater percent of success in the marriages. Many would say that the reason most marriages fail is due to the lack of love and personal spousal consideration. As such, I ask you a question: "What is it about your spouse, or intended spouse, that attracts you?" Was it that he or she was a good athlete, singer, writer, beautiful/handsome, intelligent, rich, tall, short, slim/fat, fair-skinned/tan-skinned, nice personality, political/economical type influence, or some other visible aspect? Whatever it or they were, must have caught your eye, or maybe "touched your heart." But after your initial attraction of the intended spouse, did you become alert and conscious of any of the three words of importance that are expressed in this presentation? Obviously, most of the people have not bothered themselves to become aware of "Firm, Fair and Consistent," in reference to the spousal character considerations.

In my tripartite management process, I have not yet mentioned the sure importance of a certain word and its concept, of which most people connect to the marital process. That is the word, "love". Of course, most all people do connect "love" to the courting process and of course, finally it is supposedly affirmed in the matrimonial action. However, one should understand that it will take a while through observation of the intended one to be sure of him/her. A "whirlwind" engagement is in danger for failure. I believe, like most others do believe, that love is a very important ingredient for the success of a marriage. However, my point here is to establish, "What is it that initially attracts people to each other and after the consummation of the ceremony, what is it that maintains the marriage over a long period of time?" Maybe all of us can understand this concept; if someone exhibits various positive characteristics, those will cause a likely tendency for others to demonstrate affection, or love, for that person. Most people will accept that declaration.

As such, as we speak about "Firm, Fair and Consistent" as this concept is related to marriage and family, I have included this important word, "love". In these days, I have noted that in many peoples' conversations and various writings and television commercials, the use of the word "love" is presented in most cases, in a rather "loose" or degraded manner. That is, frequently they are not using it as the word was originally meant to be used, which was basically between people and not to be attached to "things of interest," in a moment of conversation. The word love was intended originally to be used with someone, or even an animal, that could respond in a similar fashion. However, inanimate objects cannot respond. "Do not love the world, nor the things in the world." (1 John 2:15) (Bible- Recovery Version)

In other words, love was used originally as an "interactive" word, which suggested that the so-called "object" of the applied love, was living and could potentially respond to the expression of love toward it. Notice should be taken that, as a reference in the Bible, Jesus said, "The love of money is the root of all evil." (1Tim 6:10) So, I say that, since money is an inanimate object, it actually cannot "respond" to anyone, at least not as one person to another. Most people do not understand that money is just another "tool," among many that are available, to do something or get something done that we need. Neither do other inanimate objects have the capacity or ability to respond to us, such as, our automobile, house, clothes, occupation, the weather and even food we <u>enjoy</u>.

<u>We respond</u>, as living creatures, to various objects and things, which are a part of our environment, but they do not respond to us. It appears that most people are deceived, because when money or some other behavior is used to get a <u>result</u>, most interpret it as a <u>response</u>. Based on that understanding,

if they are happy with that result, they experience a pleasant or happy feeling and tend to use the word "love" to express the feeling, which, in my interpretation, is inappropriate. As such, we should concentrate on placing love, which is "intimate affection," on "we the people," who are animated, living and responding creatures. With this kind of an understanding, and applying it in the "Firm, Fair and Consistent" management process, I believe that practically any person can have a very successful living, in marital/family and social situations.

Of course, when we produce a baby and have a growing child, it is easy to love that child. This is mainly because the child is part of us, but also, the child has not yet done anything to offend, hurt or disgrace us. However, take this into consideration and even understanding it; that even though human love is a positive emotion, it can be changeable and mercurial in nature. And that is most likely when one's own situation, for matrimonial or other cases, does not turn-out like it was expected to be from the beginning. Hence, it is important for the spouses to have at least a few enduring and positive characteristics, along with the love, such as the three important character words in this presentation. These can be similar to a type of matrimonial cement or glue, which could help to hold together and even maintain a marriage and family, in order to overcome "trials and tribulations."

As stated earlier, these three words, as character traits in the spouses, help give each other a feeling of confidence, security and some degree of comfort in the daily trials and difficulties that can occur in a marriage and family. This is extremely important, in that a married couple has its various expectations of happiness and blissful times. But, most of us are quite aware that marriage has its difficult times, which test our fortitude for overcoming the times of "trials and tribulations." Hopefully, the couple would come out of them even stronger and more mature than before. However, this aspect of the relationship would depend on what kind of "glue" there is in the marriage that is significant enough, in order to maintain the marriage. That is, how <u>consistently</u> are they dedicated to be Firm and Fair in the relationship, in order to maintain it? As such, it is quite important for each of the spouses to seriously consider, before marriage, what kind of characteristics each of them has in their personalities. Doing this could possibly prevent a marital "wreck" in the future, or at least prevent some uncomfortable and very irritating situations. However, it is obvious that many marriages were consummated without consideration of what is suggested here. In these cases, it would be necessary for at least one of the spouses, if not both, to have at least one or more of these key character traits and the need to apply them to correct and save the course of the marriage. Of course, this also will have some type of effect on any children that are produced during the marriage.

Now, the question arises about how does FFC apply to the up-bringing and guidance, as well as the training of the children within the family structure? This information and its application to the process of child-rearing are very important to the present family situation. Also, it is important for the future of the general social environment. I believe that we adults can all testify that we have seen at least some degree of decline and/or decadence in the quality of our USA society at large, and much of it being attributable to many deviant youth. It would seem logical to assume that much of the deviant behaviors that we are seeing in our neighborhoods today are due to improper child-rearing and/or a pure lack of it.

I must say that with my many years of work experience in the field of Psychology, that I have witnessed much of that poor child care and up-bringing. I do not say that all those parents functioned as "poor parents," on purpose. Most of them are apparently functioning in that manner due to ignorance. I say that, because it also seems logical to assume that no parent actually wishes to have a deviant or criminal child. Therefore, it is clear that all parents should take the responsibility of informing themselves of proven management techniques, for the adequate and proper rearing of their children. Yes, I know that most parents are usually just mainly aware of how they were brought-up in their home and use that experience as a guideline for managing their children. In such cases, the use of the management system that they would employ may be adequate, only if it actually worked well for their own up-bringing. And if not applicable, then they are back to "square one," for finding the best method for their children's upbringing. Basic positive child management should not change, just because of our new or changing technology in more "modern times."

In dealing with little children, it needs to be emphasized that we need to keep in mind that they are just naturally "egocentric" as neophytes. They just want to have what they perceive as "pleasing" to them and to avoid what to them is "distasteful." This being the case, the proper parenting process requires plenty of patience and a caring attitude, in order to be "successful," as it meets your definition of success. It is also important for parents to understand and manage the children according to all the various and different types of child personalities, with which they may be privileged to witness in their family. That is, because of the varying distribution of genetic inheritance factors and child developmental maturing progress. These types of influential factors in personality need to be considered in the management process.

The main emphasis in child management for the younger children is to establish rules and guidelines that are appropriate and <u>Fair</u> for the age and functioning level of each child. In other words, if you did have two or more of them to manage, then the idea of "one rule for all," is not likely appropriate or Fair for one or more of them at a particular time period.

That could provoke one or more of them, usually one of the younger ones, to say something like, "Why can he do that and then you don't let me do it." One of the best ways to answer that comment is to indicate that, each of them is "special" and that each one has his certain rules <u>at different ages</u>. You could say that on his next birthday, or a bit later he would be allowed to do something. Additionally, most children cannot always communicate what they are thinking or understand, but they learn at a very early age about family and social "ins and outs," and learn what works to "manipulate" a given situation for their desire or liking. Some do it by smiling and playing "cute," others by just crying and others by having a screaming tantrum.

All these types of child strategies do not actually classify them as "bad children" or "mean-spirited." They are simply immature and have not matured enough in all the necessary areas, in order to function as we would like to see them, eventually in the "adult world." In situations where there are multiple children, it may be good to remind them that, "When you are (at a certain age in question), then you can go, do, or have certain things." With that kind of management, in a multiple child-care type situation, it can be helpful to the child if he can look forward to his next birthday, for the joyful advancement to his next expectation level, like for acquiring another desired toy, activity or privilege.

Another very important aspect of child management is the application of the principles of <u>Firm and Consistent</u>. For example, no matter how good a rule may be for the guidance and care of a child; if it is not applied firmly and quite consistently, it will likely be inadequate and/or invalid. In this case of firmness and consistency, it is difficult to differentiate between them, not that it would be actually necessary to do so. Firmness, in establishing a rule, is good but if it is not applied consistently, then that will likely encourage the child to always test that rule, at least once in a while. It is an age-old rule of gambling, that if you win just once in a while and get what you want, you will likely keep-on trying again and again. But, if the parents are both equally <u>Firm and Consistent</u> in the application of the stated rule or the established guide lines, eventually the child will learn that it is a losing proposition to go against the rule.

Hence, this is the way eventually to get the children to comply with the established guidelines for this type of child management process; "Firm, Fair and Consistent" procedures applied regularly. Granted it takes a lot of patience and much determination to be Consistent and Firm in applying these guidelines. But the positive results will be worth the effort. The area of consistency is where most parents have a failure. So, the parents should know of this necessity when they decide to have children. As the Ranch Boss says: "You should have known this when you signed on here!" As such, it should be obvious for how important it is to be "informed." Being so informed as much as possible can help significantly in reducing errors in judgment and all that can help reduce some irritation and/or frustration in the management process. So, I say to you, "Be informed and not alarmed!" Hopefully, those who are reading this now, are being helped in this manner and will utilize it and profit from it.

Chapter Three

PERSONAL/SOCIAL APPLICATIONS

WHAT DO YOU THINK ABOUT when you present yourself in public? I think that most of us do not ponder very much on that subject, unless of course, we are in the process of preparing for a special occasion or event. It appears to me that in most common situations, where one goes out into the "public domain," there is no strict consideration of how one is dressed or what time of day it is. However, now days, I have seen some rather bizarre appearances by the younger crowd, in public society. In fact, some that I have seen presented themselves as if they had no "shame" about their ragged, weird or peculiar self-presentation. As many of the older crowd might think; "Wow! How the social standards and attitudes have changed!" And as we can surely see, obviously they have changed, noticeably, even with some older ones.

Aside from the younger generation's personal presentation, I think most of us are generally interested in presenting and preserving a rather "decent" type of reputation, both of appearance and conduct. Based on that assumption, we need to look at the group of habits and character traits that are exhibited by most or all of us. That group will likely determine how we are perceived by others and even calibrate the type and extent of perceptions by our family, job associates and our friends in social relationships. One way that we can get at least a rough idea of how we compare to others in our society, is to do a self-assessment with a standard and established psycho-social assessment instrument. Of course, in answering the questions and statements, one must be very honest, to the best of one's ability. The manner suggested is mentioned in the paragraph below.

If you consider the friends and associates with whom you have contact and the types of relationships you have with each one, you will begin to understand how you have used or not applied the terms, "Firm, Fair and Consistent," to your family, vocational and social types of relationships. First, one should render a type of self-assessment of how successful is each relationship (of course, this is a subjective opinion). In my profession as a Psychologist for many years, I have relied on the MMPI instrument to help me assess various individuals, both those of deviant character and those who are basically "normal" individuals. As mentioned, if you were to complete that instrument, being very honest, you might learn some new kinds of information about yourself. In doing that, it will become fairly clear as to what kinds or types of strategies you have used in relating to others. From this assessment of yourself, assuming that you have been honest in doing so, you will be able to determine if and/or when you have exhibited any of the characteristics of "Firm, Fair or Consistent" in your present relationships. This would be especially helpful for you if one or more of these relationships are not going as "smoothly" as you would like, so as to gain ideas, or strategies, that would likely help in the improving of your relationships.

Now, with a true personal assessment, you would have a base from which to begin working on the situation, by truthfully assessing your behavior or your conduct in each of those relationships. In saying this and presenting this type of process for your personal improvement of relationships, it is assumed that you, or any other person being considered, is of relatively "sound mind" and can think and reason normally. As could be assumed, it would be ridiculous for us to expect that most psychologically deficient persons could do an accurate assessment of their own personal situation, as it has been described, in order to make some notable improvements. In reference to a Fair personal assessment, one should examine his "personal identity" (ID) in a variety of settings or situations.

First, what is your ID in your family setting? How are you viewed and/or perceived in that environment? Next, what is your ID in your educational setting and later in your work environment? Now, in general, how are you viewed, or thought of in your social setting? Maybe, you think of this as your "reputation". You may be viewed simply as a laborer, a teacher, or as a salesman, carpenter, preacher, seamstress, or a professor and book author, etc. Whatever your personal, social/vocational IDs are, they should be used in this kind of personal assessment of how you "stand," in reference to your relationships, with those whom you associate. In doing so, one can use this information of FFC to look at what influence, or lack of it, that the use of these character traits could have on your idea of good, bad or mediocre relationships in any of the areas mentioned. This point is emphasized in that, one's ID is certainly important in these settings.

One way for anyone to assess how his relationship toward others, with whom he has social or familial contact, is to consider how he would expect those "others" to relate to him. One aspect that is very common for most people is, "If I expect that others should respect me, then I also need to show respect toward them." That is touching on the word, Fair. In other areas of social relationships there are other types of considerations, such as moral/ethical standards. For most adults, it is understood that in certain places and under certain social type situations, one should do or not do certain things, or exhibit certain behaviors. Yes, I know that in these days, there has been notable laxity in using behavioral constraint by some people now, especially in these current political street rallies. But, for most of us, we are more constrained in our social behavior and therefore, more Firm in our manner of comportment. That, in itself, is a good start in successful living.

The two words of Firm and Consistent are very closely related. For example in our work routine, most all "good employees" are consistent in reporting to the work site on time each work day. Also, "good renters" or "good product buyers" usually pay their bills regularly and on time. These are common and every-day types of examples, which demonstrate the word Consistent. However, for people to demonstrate that they are Consistent in doing anything, they must be very Firm in their true commitment to do so, on a regular basis. That is, they truly believe in doing it, because they are convinced that it is the "right thing" to do. It then becomes one of their character traits, that which is consistently exhibited. These character traits, to which we are referring and discussing, are not due to something with which we were born, or which were miraculously bestowed upon us; but they are acquired through practice and more practice, over time, until they become "ingrained" habits as part of us.

And now, as we grow and hopefully mature, both physically and personally, we surely must learn that we need to adjust and do some accommodating in our various environments.

That will mean various things to various people, in various types of environments. In general terms, we know that for most of us, it could mean that in certain places, we will be expected to dress in a certain fashion, or to behave in a certain manner, or to do certain things at a certain time, etc. Those are some of the most difficult things that young people have to learn as they are maturing. The main reason is that, most young people have not yet fully "out-grown" those egocentric tendencies of childhood, which were mentioned earlier, and tend to resist things and situations that feel uncomfortable, or seem a bit distasteful to them. Unfortunately, some adults still retain and express some of these egocentric tendencies, which impede their appropriate adjustment.

As most adults have observed with young people, many of them exhibit the natural human tendency to just "act on impulse" or, to do something just because "I feel like it." Obviously, this negates any thought of acting consistently in a positive way. Perhaps this is also somewhat internally promoted, due to a considerable amount of youthful excess energy, which needs to be expended. In all my years in the fields of teaching, coaching and counseling youth, I cannot recall any of the youth speaking or commenting positively about developing any certain positive habits. Of course, the football players understood that they had to practice and practice the plays, so that they could execute them very well in a game situation. However, I believe that most of them did not think of how this principle applies to every-day types of living situations and the requirements of family and daily educational and social functioning situations.

This is the point of interest here, in that we need "good teachers" in all areas; such as, in coaching situations, school teachers, politicos, business leaders, business bosses, parents and even our grandparents. In saying this, I would also emphasize that it would be good for our youth, attending many USA colleges and universities, if many of the professors were not so intent on promoting their "progressive/socialistic" type of agendas in the classrooms. In saying this, the implication is that in all areas of our living, the leaders in their particular areas of experience and/or "expertise," should do the best that they can to teach, instruct, or lead the younger and less experienced people to develop good and positive habits, which would be exhibited on a Consistent basis. This should be done strictly and without promoting some sort of hidden political agenda (or even not hidden sometimes).

That which should be obvious to all, is that most of the behavior problems and lack of successful social functioning, as youth are developing, mostly could be avoided from the beginning with Consistent and appropriate parenting practices. I remember some of the older folks, upon viewing some youngsters, behaving inappropriately and saying, "They had some poor up-bringing." This applies to what I said just now about how proper home-training could avoid much of the improper family and social behavior problems, which are quite prevalent today. So, it does behoove all of us who are rational, caring adults, to help in the area of promoting the Consistent use of positive behaviors, not only of our own children, but with others and including some of the adults. This not only would help us personally to have a smoother living situation, but it also can contribute positively to others' social lives as well, especially if it is done in a smooth and affable manner. We all should remember that "truth and rightness," although they are wonderful to have in our lives, are not always easily acquired or, easily included in a situation, scenario, or the environment.

Mainly, in reference to the manner that those concepts may be accepted or resisted, it will depend on the manner in which they are presented to those who are involved. As such, it is important for us, who wish to promote positive FFC concepts, to do so in the most positive and palatable manner that we can find, for possible success. In this situation, "following the path of least resistance," would appear to increase the probability of being successful. I mean that in a positive manner; that is, to promote FFC in the least "uncomfortable or painful" manner, for most people. Using this type of approach, I have found that it seems to work quite well, if the reason for applying these principles is explained simply and concisely, especially with young children and the youth. No long explanations are needed, nor are they very well accepted by most people. So, we should be concise and direct, but presenting our ideas, rules and guidelines in a smooth and congenial manner. Of course, dealing with our young children in our home can be a more challenging situation, in that we must be very sure that we implement this system in a very "Firm, Fair and Consistent" manner.

Chapter Four

EDUCATIONAL AND VOCATIONAL APPLICATIONS

WHO IS ADEQUATELY EDUCATED? AND, what would that indicate for us who think that we are adequately educated? Probably, most of us have had at least one situation, where we had an experience of entering into a new job setting and having a feeling of anxiousness and/or insecurity, for what machinations may be awaiting us. And sure enough, there always seem to be at least one or more of these situations that were not covered in our education or training process. As such, we can see that formal education most usually gives an emphasis on <u>giving</u> us information, which pertains to the certain areas that we are mandated to learn in public schools, or that we have chosen in colleges. However, when we go out into the world of work there is the need to <u>apply</u> the information that we have gathered in the educational process. But, there may be some situations in our jobs where it appears that what we were taught does not "fit" or apply very well in those certain situations. That is when "Firm and Consistent" should appear in our repertoire, for remediation of the situation.

Well now, I ask you another question. In your educational process did you learn and/or develop some certain "facts of life" that pertain to your character building, besides just acquiring some factual information? If you did, I would hope that an attitude of Firm persistence was attained. This is related to the attitude commonly referred to as "Don't give-up." That is, if something you have tried did not work, or did not work as well as desired, then try modifying the approach to the situation or, try a different method, but not "giving-up".

I have heard of similar situations that have caused one participant to decide to invent something that will work well. One case was initiated because of his frustration with a home alarm apparatus, which was too much trouble to install, because of needing to put wires everywhere and other problems of installation. As such, he developed a wireless type home alarm system and has profited well from it. In this case, he was quite determined to realize his desire to have a less complicated device to fulfill a perceived need and did so by being Firm and quite Consistent in his persistence. Of course, this is just one specific case, but it shows how we can use our knowledge and skills in positive ways to accomplish our goals; that is, if we are Consistently Firm and persistent in our efforts.

For sure, not all of the situations of difficulty that we may encounter can be resolved by us immediately. However, if the situation is one that is absolutely necessary to be resolved, then we, who have freely developed a characteristic of "will-strength" and persistence, will consult with someone else, who may give us a solution. In every difficult situation, in need of resolution, it mostly depends on how strongly you are motivated to solve the problem. A strong motivation tends to produce a Firm persistence and perseverance. I say again, this is not something with which we are endowed with at birth, or that is bestowed upon us, like by someone, as like a "miracle." We are talking about that which is installed into our character, by practicing certain behaviors again and again, until they become habits that are absorbed into our character. This is what I call, "good living."

I would like to think that my counseling of youth over many years has helped them to develop character traits of "Firm, Fair and Consistent." And with the thousands of youth that I have counseled and evaluated, I do have at least a few of them who have reportedly improved their lives and have become, as we say, "decent citizens." I appreciate that situation and how problematic youth have improved their lives by taking responsibility for successful living. I also think of how those who do not have any serious problems, could be people with a more successful living, and/or could be enjoying their living situation more by the employment of this personal management process of "Firm, Fair and Consistent," into their living situation.

I noted recently that a school district in Texas (ECISD) had begun their version of a "behavior improvement" program, to help reduce discipline behavior referrals in middle schools. This process is initiated by some of the middle school students teaching their peers about leadership through, "The 7 Habits of Highly Effective Teens" program. This is their version of a type of program that actually does incorporate the tenets of FFC, without using the actual words that are used in this presentation. The development of the proper personal characteristics in youth suggest a much more positive probability of them having more successful educational, vocational and social endeavors as they mature. However, at this point, I wish to make this short statement. If these here mentioned middle school children and others mentioned in this book, had been parented adequately, in their up-bringing years, there would likely be no need for their school program, or for mine either. I believe we all could agree on that.

Another good example is that being Firm and Consistent certainly is useful for youths to finish high school and then go on to graduate from college, or some type of special vocational training. Then as stated, entering the world of work, those types of character traits are quite useful to maintain one's employment status and to even improve one's progress in the chosen vocation. As adults, if most of us had taken this path, it is likely that we would have had much fewer educational, social and vocational problems. In practicing these mentioned habits over a fairly long time period, we would not only absorb them into our person, as some personal characteristics, but we would also note that we would start to apply them to the other areas of our life, not just education or vocation. This would improve our living situation and could be a good example to others.

Alas, most of us did not have access to the information presented here about this tripartite process of "Firm, Fair and Consistent." However, it is never too late for one to be convinced of acquiring a more "Firm, Fair and Consistent" type of attitude, that is, if one truly is <u>convinced</u>. And as I have indicated, in this presentation, if one truly is convinced about anything and consistently pursues the goal, then, the traits mentioned here will eventually be forthcoming to be supportive of the desire for the accomplishing of any given goal. This is what I and many others would classify as "successful living." And who does not wish to have a very highly successful living? I would assume that all of us would desire "success" at all levels in our lives. This is another important point, on which I believe that we all can agree!

Chapter Five

GOVERNMENTAL/POLITICAL APPLICATIONS

THIS AREA THAT WE NOW consider, in some way or another, actually touches everyone in the USA, as well as, even some people in the international realm. How much we are touched, would be according to how much involvement we have with the various levels of our types of government, like: Federal, State, County (Parish in Louisiana), City. As such, this situation puts us in a position to have at least some minimal contact with laws, rules and those regulations that govern our daily lives. In fact, we also must deal with the results of those elected officials who make those laws, rules and regulations; and also, the usual Federal, State, County and local Police forces, who enforce them and the Judicial branch, that interprets and judges on the court cases involving any transgressions of all those kinds of governmental statutes and regulations.

Wow! When you put all that together, it stands to reason why so many retirees and many others are starting to leave the USA and retire overseas. At least two or three reputable organizations do good international research for the purpose of discovering the "best overseas type retirement countries and cities." In some way or another, this tells me that there are plenty of USA citizens who are not happy with the way our governments are functioning and affecting their lives. And some of them took "exit-action." I believe that the recent Presidential Election revealed that the majority of those who voted were unhappy and even angry with the past Federal Congress and Administration. It was mainly because they did not do what they stated, in their campaign promises and promotions. As it is said, they were "All Talk and no Walk." The positive is, "Walk the Talk."

As such, we come to the point where the people perceive that there is an inconsistency by the elected "politicos," having a duty to serve "We the People," and they are not doing a good job, at least not consistently. It seems that most of these elected officials, when confronted with their not completing something as they promised, use the excuse of saying that, "We cannot always get our way. We have to compromise." To some extent that may be true, but many are not Consistent and Firm, in their efforts to be Fair to those who elected them to be responsible for what they promised or promoted in their election campaigns.

Now with that thought in mind, let us consider what appears to be a rather large gap between what a notable number of elected officials "<u>say</u> they will do" and "*what* they <u>actually do</u>." It has been long noted that there have been many well-intentioned elected officials, who have gone into Federal Congress and/or State Legislatures and do some good initial work. However, it seems that after a couple of terms in office, a notable number of them start to "waver" in their due dedication to the basic honorable principles that they initially promoted. Based on my observations and those of others also, it appears that some politicians have the idea of becoming a "career" politician, which becomes prevalent in the minds of those elected officials. Of course, this definitely <u>was not the intention</u> of our Founding Fathers of this USA nation. But as such, this has become prevalent over many decades and has much influence for causing many governmental problems, which we can see are quite prevalent. One of the problematic examples now follows.

For many years our USA Congress, and various others, have talked about and made promises about doing something to control and/or remedy the problem of our so-called "national debt," which is now over $22 Trillion dollars! However, the ones in Congress, who can do something about it, seem to forget about promises made during their campaigns for office.

The question then should follow as such: "Are you being 'Firm, Fair and Consistent' in what you promised to do about our national debt?" It never gets reduced any and instead, keeps growing each year. We not only need to hold ourselves accountable for the way we conduct our own life situations, but we also need to pay attention to our political "servants," who are supposed to be representing us, "We the People," in a positive manner. That is, we not only need to observe them closely, but force accountability from them and if they fail to comply, vote them out of office!

Why? You may ask. Well, it seems very clear to me and others, that when political officials have become concerned frequently, (each 4/6 years, and even during their present term), about their re-election, there arises a problem. The reason is that, the officials are tempted and are likely to do things in their favor, which are directed toward helping re-election, instead of their being dedicated and Consistent in serving "We the People." Of course, one of the courses of action that could help eliminate much of this problem is to have "term limits," imposed on the Congress. The law indicates that the Presidency is limited at two terms and it should be clear to the people that, now they should demand this for the Congress also. This kind of lawful regulation would be in line with what our Founding Fathers had intended. They would be serving as "statesmen" for one or two terms and then, return to their own home and working situation. As such, it would mean that they would return to being as one of us, "We the People."

Based on that information, it can be accurately stated that it is necessary that our governmental elected officials not only need to see and to understand this, but they need to conform to it now! If we elect Senators or Representatives based on their good qualities (such as FFC) and if they know that they only have two terms they can serve, it is more likely that they will be true to what they have promised and promoted in their campaigns. Now with unlimited terms, there is too much of the negative temptation to establish, or to get involved in, "a good-old-boy" type of network, which promotes their re-election strategies and does distract them in concentrating on adequate service to and for, "We the People."

The law was passed by Congress to limit the Presidency to only two terms. So, it appears that, in order to be Consistent and Fair to both branches of the government, we should insist that this type of law should be applied as well, to all members of our U.S. Congress. Also, it is my opinion that even the Supreme Court justice terms should be limited to 10 years. Yes, I know that may be a bit controversial, but having a lifetime type of appointment seems too much. This is especially needed if there is one or more on the Court who believe that our US Constitution is a "living and breathing" type document and it should be flexible, so as to be "changeable," according to the opinion of those so-called "progressive" judges. If the justices would have done a good job in their 10-year term, then they could be nominated to have another term and be confirmed by the Senate.

Otherwise, with lifetime terms for federal judges, this type of situation may amount to some judges attempting to "legislate" instead of doing their job to "adjudicate." In a few cases, this seems to have happened. Our Founding Fathers formed a wonderful US Constitution and it has endured over 200 years! This should give a strong and meaningful message to those who promote the type of progressive attitude about our Constitution, being something that could be an easily "altered document," by the opinions of judges. Making changes in the laws that cover all the changes that may be needed in our society's stand on morals, ethics and our economy, should be left to the working responsibility of our U.S. Congress and state Legislatures. Recently, in his election pledge in campaigning for President, Donald Trump said, "We will drain the swamp." This is an intention to get rid of the "old cronies," who have been "doing politics as usual," for a long time. I simply say, "Good luck" and I hope he is "Firm, Fair and Consistent" in his process of doing so! This may be a good wake-up call for all political workers. At least, there is a need to "shake-up" Washington, D.C.! And I believe that we all know that D.C. needs a good "shaking," even at the risk of strong opposition from those so-called, "swamp dwellers"!

As has been indicated in other sections of this book, for anyone to be a politician and determined in the pursuit of being "Firm, Fair and Consistent," that person needs to be one who has acquired and absorbed those traits into his character, <u>before</u> entering into the political arena. If that person has not shown a history of his exhibiting these qualities before he is elected, then we cannot truly expect that these will be developed in the trying political process, due to the various temptations as mentioned. As such, <u>voters beware!</u> And take an active interest in the electoral voting process to validate as to whether the candidate, for whom you vote, basically has exhibited the positive characteristics that are mentioned here. Can you imagine how great our USA Congress and the various Legislatures would function, if all the voters would seriously take a close look at the very responsible task of "vetting" each candidate that they are considering in the election process? Yes, I know that this takes a bit more time to do some research and in a busy lifestyle, many believe it to be inconvenient to do. But if this would be done more <u>Consistently and Firmly</u>, by the majority of the voters, that kind of election voting surely would elect more good and responsible officials, giving us a much fresher/cleaner/higher quality of a governmental and political result! As such, we all would profit in many and varied ways.

Chapter Six

SPIRITUAL CONSIDERATIONS/
APPLICATIONS

AND NOW, WE ARE ENTERING into a highly controversial area of our lives, in the discussion and presentation of information in this section of this book. And I say this because there are even more diverse ideas, opinions, beliefs and non-beliefs in this area of our lives, than in the other areas that we have previously reviewed. As such, in the beginning Preface, I gave to you a synopsis of my biographical and spiritual background, so that from the beginning of this writing, you would see and maybe understand "from where I am coming." We all have our orientations from the time we were born and on into adulthood. As such, that is primarily the base from which we derive our perceptions, beliefs and personal life-skills for our present personal functioning. Therefore, since my basic orientation in this area is founded on my Christian beliefs, I will present my findings related to this subject area, based on what I see and believe are in the biblical Scriptures, as the various types of examples for the management system of "Firm, Fair and Consistent." As stated before, the biblical quotations given are of the Recovery Version (203).

From the very beginning of today's mankind (man), being formed in the image and likeness of God (Genesis 1:26), I believe that God's purpose was to develop creatures (humans) to represent Him and to express Him, in the form of his personal image and likeness, on this Earth and in this vast Universe, which He created. But as the story goes in the Scriptures, Lucifer, the "head-angel" at that time, rebelled and became the enemy of God, with a large number of other (1/3 of all) angels. Lucifer came to Eve as a serpent and tempted her (Genesis 3:1-7). Lucifer, who is known as Satan, goes against what God does and desires, tempting all of mankind in various subtle ways, to deviate them from God's plan. God, being Firm as He is, told Adam and Eve from the beginning about what He expected of them, especially in reference to the two trees in the garden. He explained what the two main trees represented in the Garden of Eden. God said to the man and woman, "Of every tree of the garden you may eat freely, but of the tree of the knowledge of good and evil, of it you shall not eat; for in the day that you eat of it you shall die" (Genesis 2:16-17). God did give the man and woman a free will, so they could make choices of what they wished to do or not to do, in any situation. But, He also gave them a clear warning of consequences that would come to them, if they should eat from the "forbidden tree."

I certainly do not know the answer to this question; "Did Adam and Eve know and understand the concept of dying or death?" But I am sure that most of us know what happened, following Eve's eating of the fruit from the "forbidden tree" and also giving it to Adam. This caused mankind to "fall into a permanent <u>sinful condition</u>." As such, the two of them became one, in a sinful condition. That is man's condition as a permanent one, unless they "turn to God," by their accepting Jesus, the Christ and Son of God, as their redemption and salvation, in order to escape perdition. In that fallen condition the creatures naturally produced their offspring like themselves, mainly expressing their fallen selves, instead of fulfilling the true desire of God; that is to express Him. The situation being as such, God, as we even may naturally say, "has had His hands full," to deal with man's "fallen condition" and to recover a "few men" for His purpose on Earth. As such, He is still working now on man's "recovery process" in today's world.

Now that we have that background established, as a setting and base for the rest of the presentation in this section, I wish to explain what I understand about that part of Genesis 1:26, which I see as extremely important about this tripartite process. And it mainly is the basis for the writing of this book. That part of the verse in Genesis, "image and likeness," is the basis for the terms used here, "Firm, Fair and Consistent." May we have an open mind to truly look at this phraseology, for investigating and understanding; what does it truly mean for us, as human beings? I believe that if anyone truthfully can say that he is functioning as "Firm, Fair and Consistent," he should look clearly to God Almighty, because He truly functions as such! In fact, where do you think we, as human beings, have observed the good example of this type of functioning over the many centuries of our existence on Earth? God has given us excellent examples as a good "role model." Now, I will give you an explanation of my belief and understanding of the phrase, of which I previously indicated as, "image and likeness." This is crucial for all of us in our understanding of who we are and what we are!

When God formed man "from the dust of the Earth," (Genesis 2:7) this was to form a type of physical being, in the "image" of His Person, that is, an image of His Person as the Invisible One. God the Father, the Creator, is an invisible Figure and we, the physical creatures, cannot see Him, but it is obvious by the Scriptures that He has an image (Genesis 1:26), or He would not have said so. Therefore, when He formed man from the dust of the Earth and woman from the man's rib, He desired that His earthly and universal representatives should be made in His own "image and likeness". One can understand this concept by observing what happens in quite a multitude of cases, every day on this Earth, with births of human beings. When we have a child, surely we wish to have a child born in our own image and not, for example, a child in the image of a dog or a monkey or a cow, or something other than a real human being! Image indicates a "form" of some kind and in this case we are speaking about the image of God, which is in the form that He has referred to as "man." God made the first man in a perfect image of Himself, but these first images of mankind became defiled, due to being overcome with temptation from God's enemy, Satan. And Satan is still working constantly today, in an attempt to delay his destiny, for the lake of fire, as long as he can. This is done by Satan in many subtle ways, in order to distract us and to do so, even sometimes, with influences from so-called "good things."

However, when we have children, we expect them to be in our own image. So, not being perfect, how can we expect our child to be a "perfect one?" Well, none of us is perfect, at least, not until we go through the God-Ordained process of redemption, regeneration of our spirit, transformation of our soul, and last, the transfiguration of our old physical body in the "last day." (Phil 3:21) That is, the complete and final "recovery process" for our full salvation! The process takes a fairly long time to complete and is the reason that God has given most of us a 70-year time-span, or even to 80 years or more, (that is, if we take good care of what He has given us, our body), to figure-out and understand what He desires of us. Next, there comes the time of judgement for all of us. That is necessary to see at what level we have functioned, in doing the will of God, during our tenure on Earth. There are many on this Earth who do not believe any of what I am saying; but no matter, because all human beings will come before the Judgement Seat of Christ (2 Cor. 5:10), to be "reviewed," whether they believe it or not! So therefore, I say, take heed and seek the will of God Almighty for your well-being now and also in eternity!

Therefore God, in His inimitable way, formed us in His own image and likeness, for His expression. It is thought and believed by most Christians and others, that God <u>created</u> our man-type physical form, but not so. The Scripture plainly states that, "Jehovah God formed man from the dust of the ground and breathed into his nostrils the breath of life, and man became a living soul." (Genesis 2:7) The <u>creation</u> portion of our existence occurred, when immediately after the physical part was <u>formed</u>. That was when our God "breathed the breath of life" into man, <u>creating</u> the soul and human spirit, inside the physical body that he had just <u>formed</u>. The Holy Spirit was not yet given. I hope we all can understand this and that we can appreciate it, as our beginning on this God-created Earth. We will touch on this particular subject a bit later in this presentation.

Now we will investigate the other important word in this section, which is "likeness". Using the Random House dictionary again, we look at one of the few explanations of this word. It indicates that the word "likeness" may be rendered as, "a state or fact of being like" something or someone. Also, there are two other words given, "resemblance & similitude." When we use the word "like" and are referring to someone, we usually mean that the person is favored by us or, that the person possibly, "looks like someone else." However, here in the biblical sense, using the word "likeness," we are speaking in terms of much more than in the physical sense, or possibly in the sense of "likeability." We are referring to God in such a manner, for lack of a better terminology, as His natural being. It refers to who He is as the Supreme Being in the Universe, His characteristics.

For sure, some of His characteristics include, "Firm, Fair and Consistent," among various others. If anyone has read/ studied the Bible, it should become evident that God is "Firm," strong, steady, dependable and trustworthy in what He says and promises. This is quite evident over the many centuries of history that is recorded in the Bible by various prophets, apostles and the Lord Jesus Christ. In all cases, when God makes a promise, He surely has completed it and/or will do so in the future, as the particular situation warrants it. As such, in respect to these kinds of characteristics, He desires to see His believers exhibiting the same types of characteristics.

Yes, it is obvious that we do not have the almighty power that God has, but we do have a free will, with which we can decide to complete His own word as much as humanly possible, especially with His help. As a matter of fact He desires that we believers should not only believe <u>in Him</u> and <u>confide in Him</u>, but also to <u>depend upon Him</u> for our daily living needs and deeds. Because God is the Ultimate in firmness and truthfulness, we can have the surety and ultimate confidence in Him, that He will always fulfill His promises and will complete His Word, which is <u>His breath and Spirit</u> (2Tim 3:16). May He always alert us and maintain us, as His believers, in this spiritual principle of truth, which is Firm, Fair and Consistent.

Now, in reference to what was mentioned previously about God's forming and creating mankind, I would like to elaborate somewhat on the three parts of man. Our God has shown a preference or consistency to represent Himself and us in a "tripartite" manner. As such, we have God the Father (Jehovah) and Creator; the Son (Jesus) as our Savior, the Christ; and the Holy Spirit, the Transmitter of all that God is and does in this universe, including what He does in us, the believers. As stated previously, God formed and created man with three parts, body, soul and human spirit. The physical body is to contain the soul and spirit of man. The soul is composed of the <u>mind, emotion and will</u>. And the human spirit includes the <u>conscience, intuition and fellowship</u>

modalities, or functions. As you can see, there is a tripartite parallel in our creation established and as such, it gives us another example of God's consistency in His process of all creation. In this, I also followed this process, in using these main words of, "Firm, Fair and Consistent," which are crucial elements in all situations of our lives and our destinies.

Not only is our God known for His Firm spiritual/practical principles, but He is well known for being Fair in all aspects. That is, that He is "just" in making His decisions concerning all human beings, and even in judging Satan. Unfortunately for Satan, with his rebellious angels and evil spirits, they have their just destiny in the "lake of fire." Those of the human race, who do not choose redemption and who may even follow in Satan's pathways, in this time-limited world, will all receive the same just treatment as Satan. I surely hope that no one reading this book is in that category. We all need to remember and to realize that God made us with a free will to choose what we will do and will not do. As such, we need to also realize that we all are responsible for what we decide, both spiritually and in all of our practical living matters, which will bring positive or negative consequences.

Therefore, since God gave us a free will, it is "just" and is only "fair" that we should be rightly held responsible for the decisions that we make on a daily basis and those that we make "just once in a while." I am sure that we all would think that having a "free will" is really great, but with it comes the fact that <u>we are also responsible for our decisions</u> and we will be required to give an account for those decisions. Therefore, if we accept and believe the foregoing statements, then it is imperative that we should adjust our attitude and behaviors to <u>God's standards</u>. Otherwise, we will be required to suffer His mandatory consequences, when we are "reviewed" by God, in the last days, as Scriptures indicate (Rev 20:11-12, 15). Anyway, as it is frequently said in the world, "In this case, even if you do not believe it, what do you have to lose in trying it?" Now that you know, my good advice is, "Always be prepared!" And as such, you will not fail, but will be saved or "spared," from any "harsh judgement."

Thank God for His being "Consistent" as well as, "Firm and Fair." As we can see in His universal creation, God has everything in its place and all things that He created are simply functioning consistently as He intended. What I said was "all the things that he <u>created</u>." But you need to understand, that to "create" is to bring something into existence from nothing; that which was not formerly in existence. Remember that He "formed Adam from dust of the Earth." As such, some things, especially people, are not "functioning consistently as He intended." Actually man did not start to "age and physically decline," until sin from Satan entered his body. That gave us a condition of physical <u>degeneration</u> and a deviation, psychologically and spiritually, from God's original intention for our functioning. However, God has provided a "recovery process" of spiritual <u>regeneration</u>, by the redemption process. It was established by the sacrifice of the Lord Jesus Christ (God in the flesh of man), for the recovery of mankind, who choose to become believers in Christ Jesus, at the good pleasure of God the Father and Creator, through the Holy Spirit. The Lord Jesus was the only pure and acceptable <u>sacrifice</u> that God would accept for the redemption of sinful, fallen mankind. This was because of what He said; "without shedding of blood there is no forgiveness." (He 9:22)

As such, Jesus the Christ was crucified on a cross, died, buried and arose on the third day, as the One and Only Redeemer and Savior, for those believers in Him. God has proven that He is "Firm, Fair and Consistent" in His God-ordained way. He is Consistent in this process; and as such, this gives us believers much confidence, courage and stronger faith in Him, to carry-on in His recovery process of mankind. If you are not familiar with the term, "recovery process," I will explain its use. In the process of Satan tempting man and causing man to fall into a sinful condition, our God lost His true expression through all mankind. As such, God had to initiate a "recovery process" to give the pathway for all mankind to have a way to become a viable expression of God, the Father and Creator. The way for one to be a participant in this recovery process has been explained previously.

As practical examples of His consistency, let us consider that we have "day and night" on a Consistent basis. The seasons of the year change regularly every year. Gravity of the Earth is continual and basically Consistent in all the areas. Everyone eventually dies and is physically terminated on a Consistent basis. Even I noted that water, in its process of going down the sink drain hole, will swirl in one direction, if it is on the south side of the equator and will swirl in the opposite direction if on the north side. These are consistent principles and they never change. And furthermore, in His creation of all those things, including the very concept of "time," I hope you can see how these examples suggest, imply and even give Fair evidence of how "Consistent" our God is in all things that He created in this Universe. Although "time" is consistent, we all have a limited amount of it available to us and we will be held accountable for what we have done with it while here on this Earth.

If something might occur in your lifetime that may seem to be inconsistent and you think that it is something from God; you need to closely look at all the facts of the case and read your Bible, which is the best "reference book" that you will be able to find. This should be done in order for you to see where you are in error, or in disbelief, or just misunderstanding the true essence of your situation; because, <u>we are the inconsistent ones, not God</u>. As such, we the believers in Him need to follow His good life example, for living the true believer's life.

The simple reason that God is always Consistent in how He reviews and judges every type of situation in which we human beings are involved, is that, He desires to assure us that He also is Fair and just. Therefore, in your case or that of anyone, if you think that God must have surely made a mistake in your case; think again! By allowing something to happen or causing it to happen, God wants you to review the situation very carefully. We may be many times wrong in our own assumptions, but God is never wrong. As such, before we suggest that God has made an error in His judgement, it would behoove all of us to review our case, or situation, very closely and compare it to biblical Scripture; for a better or more accurate assessment of it, instead of "jumping to conclusions." Now, with a good biblical translation (Recovery Version), our God Almighty talks to us and we need to listen intently. It will help protect us from making judgment errors.

All of this is said in confirmation of God's consistency in dealing with all people, even the non-believers. However, in order that we should understand God's will much better, I wish to explain this aspect of His character, which I have read about in the Bible and experienced in my living. I have seen that God has two "sides or aspects" to His will. First, there is the "passive" aspect of His will, as to when He "allows" certain things and situations to happen. A biblical example of this is in the case of Job, with his many trials and tribulations. (Job 1:8-22) God "allowed" Satan to "test" Job's fidelity to God for a period of time, and it was a very difficult trial for Job, but he survived and "passed the test." The other side of

God's will is the "active" side, which is when God does make things or situations happen. An example of this aspect of His will is the case of "Sodom and Gomorra" and their total destruction, due to the extreme sinfulness that existed there. (Genesis 13:10; 19:24) This occurred after many warnings from God.

That kind of "active-will action" from God usually appears after he has made various and even many attempts, through prophets, preachers and various Christian brethren, to warn those involved in any unacceptable situation, that they must correct their sinful ways. If they do not conform to His warning, then His long-suffering patience will be exhausted and the "wrath of God" judgement descends on those undisciplined ones in question. As such, I would suggest that it is never in our best interest to question God's judgement, nor to test His patience. It is best for us to just follow His basically simple biblical guidelines for our living. By this negative example of God's "active-will," one should not think that this side of His will is only negative. Just think about and remember all the many positive things He has created. Also, remember that "All things are possible with God." On the other hand, can you imagine just how <u>much more difficult</u> it would be to live and survive in this world <u>if our God would not be "Consistent"</u> in all that He says and does? So, thank God that <u>He is very Consistent</u>, truthful, reliable, <u>Firm</u> and <u>Fair</u> in all situations, even though we may not immediately see the reason or purpose. For this reason, when we are in personal prayer, we should always ask Him to enlighten us in all that He desires of us. That is living on the "safe side."

At this point, I wish to inject a personal experience, related to the last statement above. I have written, about a "near-death" experience that I had, in a book that I published, which is set in 1988 (One Bad Night In Mexico). I had been in the church life for about 8 years at that time. However, it became apparent to me that I still did not know how to pray in such a manner as to move God to enlighten me about the reason that He "allowed" the serious incident to happen to me and my father-in-law, in a near-death experience. After two years of experiencing feelings of stress and frustration, due to my not understanding why He had allowed the situation to happen, it was finally revealed to me, what the problem was. The problem was that I prayed and asked God "why" He had allowed the incident to happen. It was the manner in which I approached God about the situation that was in error. The use of the word "why" was actually a challenging of God's decision to allow the incident to happen. I learned that when asking God about a situation, we should use the word "what," so that we are asking Him a question of "What is it you are showing me;" or "God, what do You want from me?" Asking Him in this manner in not challenging Him, but is being open to Him and ready to accept a revelation of what He desires for you and me. I believe that this type of approach in personal prayers is very important. As such, and based on my personal experience with the Lord, I say to you, blessed are those who believe in these principles.

And not only believe in them, but practice them and function in the Lord accordingly! In doing so, you will experience a much more enjoyable and fruitful way of living your life and relating to those with whom you associate. We believers all need to be covered by being in a local church expression; functioning, fellowshipping and depending on God Almighty to guide our lives. This is viewed as more of an important need for us, as we see the constant decline of the spiritual, moral, ethical and social standards, in all the societies of the countries in this world. So, now you have knowledge and it is your choice, how you will respond. The Good Lord has indicated that we, the believers in Him, are "in this world but not of this world" and as such, we need to realize this concept and live according to his teachings. (1 Jn 2:15; Rom 12:2) May the Lord bless all who read this presentation and utilize its contents.

Chapter Seven

SUMMARY AND CONCLUSIONS OF FIRM, FAIR AND CONSISTENT

AFTER ALL THE FOREGOING EXPLANATIONS and examples of FFC, the question is, "Did you actually understand what was presented?" Or on the other hand, did you read and then decide that this is basically a "fantasy-land" idea of how one may try to conduct his life and that of his family? My answer is simply that all of this information is based on many years of experience in all the areas touched upon in this presentation. Furthermore, I certainly would not present something here to you that I have not proven myself, or have not vicariously experienced it through my working with others. As another "old saying" goes, "Experience is the best teacher there is, but she surely is tough!" And when one passes through the various experiences that could be classified as "trials and tribulations," or just difficult in nature, it is not easy to forget them; but one can easily realize how valuable those are for the continuing on, or to be better informed, down the "road of life." The very good gift to us, in the area of "real-life experiences," is the fact that, we would now have "tangible evidence," and not just words and/or theory espoused by a friend, teacher or college professor.

But, there is also another side to it. There must be the usage of what we generally refer to as, "common sense." I ask you to remember the definition that I gave you earlier, of "stupidity." Many people wisely utilize their experiences to gain knowledge and to improve their choices in their process of daily living. But there are some who, regardless of the negative results of their actions, continue to repeat their various mistakes. Of course, my advice to my readers is to do the best you can in order to gain a true and valid understanding of the basic principles presented here; which should definitely improve the quality of life for you and your family, both in the daily practical aspects and the lifetime spiritual aspects of your lives. As such, when this present life is finished, we will begin another type of experience and hopefully, it will be the very positive one, on the "other side."

My next question to you is, "If you understand what is presented here, do you believe it to be true?" I think that we all probably have seen or read things that we considered as likely being true. However, some of those situations or things may not be to our liking, or may be considered as not coinciding with our present process of management, and/ or just not convenient for us. As such, in my experience, those people who are most likely to believe this presentation, or to accept it, are those who have been basically, at least, attempting to apply the basic principles presented here, before they had read this book. And then there are those who have had little or limited success in their living situation and have decided to "give it a try," in order to improve their present management process. However, I would not say that there is not likely any other management process as good as this one presented here. I simply say, "If what you are doing works well then, by all means, continue in doing what is working well for you in your particular situation." Otherwise, "What do you have to lose," in trying what I have presented here? It is good for us to keep an open mind to possibilities.

Nevertheless, the use of and incorporation of the FFC process in your present management system, could improve what you are doing to some degree. It might even "enliven" your present living situation! As such, my next question is, "If you understand and believe this FFC management process, will you try to apply it in your various living situations, such as family, educational, vocational, social, and your spiritual life?" If you have not been applying this FFC process, I realize that it would be quite difficult to try it by beginning in all those areas of your life at once. However, it would be fairly simple to start in one area, such as in the home, as a beginning. This would be a good start, as you could begin with applying these principles to yourself, in terms of how you deal with children and wife/husband. This would be like "practicing privately" in the home, before applying some of the system, out in public society.

Then later, there can be the application of the same principles in the social and vocational worlds. If you would wish to apply these principles, I am now emphasizing that you should apply these principles soon, if you have not already done so, due to the tendency of human nature to forget things of which we are not accustomed to doing on a regular basis. So, if you are so-inclined, please give these an honest trial over a reasonable amount of time. Usually, anything new in our life takes a good amount of time to establish itself, especially if you desire it to become a habit. Once we have practiced these basic principles of FFC over a fair amount of time, firmly and consistently, they will become "absorbed," into us as some very useful character traits, for our healthful and enjoyable living. Of course, the usage of these characteristics will be helpful to others also, like others with whom we have relationships. Why? You may ask. I simply say that it is very "simple logic," that when we are functioning personally better in our own living situation, we surely will be more pleasurable for others who associate with us.

The very important area for potential application for FFC, which I did not mention above, is that of the spiritual area of your life. Since I do not know you personally, I certainly do not know your particular "standing" in the spiritual area. However, I must say that, based on my living experiences over the last nearly 81 years, I believe it is the most important area for each of us. This area of our life is directly related to how we believe, think, act, and relate to others; how we relate to our God and how we generally live each day, as well as, what our future and our destiny holds for us. There is a pertinent saying that goes like this, "Get right with God and you will be right with all others." There are many old sayings that I like, because they say much, in a concise manner. However, I am **not** saying that "getting right with God" will give you a "soft-and-no-problems" type of living situation. But, it will help you to correctly resolve problems you encounter. And, it will do something for you that nothing else does and that is to allow you to live a good, healthful and earnestly meaningful life, with a guaranteed rich and joyful destiny for your future. So, may the Good Lord have mercy and compassion on all who read this book, as He allows you to see and understand the basic principles for living well, which are revealed here as "Firm, Fair and Consistent" in the Lord, our Universal God.

Chapter Eight

A FEW SUPPORTIVE POETIC APPLICATIONS

THIS SMALL CHAPTER IS DEDICATED to presenting some poetic support for the foregoing chapters' presentations. For some people, it is noted that poetic type presentations make a more poignant impression on them, about the subject that is presented, rather than just plain-text presentations. As such, these poems that follow are not only for some small amount of enjoyment, but also for support and re-enforcement of the content that has been presented in this book. It is surely hoped that you enjoy the poems that I wrote, which more concisely express most of the basic tenets that are presented in the previous "plain text" presentations.

However, the last "lengthy poem" (**The Time That Made Me, Me**), which I added, is a <u>contrast</u> with the other presented poems and contents. It is not supportive of the tenets that I have shown in this book, for encouraging a more healthful, fruitful and meaningful life, but it is given in <u>worldly contrast</u> to what I have expressed here in this book. The poem basically is a lament over the poor changes in USA social status, compared to years past. But it fails to emphasize the great need we have of social, personal and spiritual "recovery" of God in our lives. May we all see this need and do our part now in God's "recovery process"! May you enjoy varying emphases on these subjects we have addressed in this book.

LIFE OF FIRM, FAIR AND CONSISTENT
(Dedicated to all mankind)

What a wonderful world it would be,
If in it, everywhere we could see,
Goodness and laughter for us to hold;
Where love and kindness each day unfold.

But alas, there is much to hinder
That Life, no matter what your gender.
So, beware and always insistent
For Life of, Firm, Fair, Consistent.

Our Life should be Firm for benefit.
For what more reasons do we live it?
Our loved ones appreciate firmness
And character expressed in earnest.

All of us like to be seen as Fair.
It shows that for others we do care.
Furthermore, it shows that we are just.
And to live in peace, this is a must.

Now, we come to the word Consistent,
To which "natural man" is resistant.
Our nature is to do whatever,
And impulsively at whenever.

So living Life, Firm, Fair, Consistent,
Even though we may be resistant,
Will require some guidance from above,
Filled with Spiritual strength and with love!

All this may seem to be rather strange,
But accept it and Life rearrange,
To enjoy a more wonderful world
For you, the secret is now unfurled!

TRUTH AND REALITY
(Dedicated to all mankind)

Viewing Truth and Reality, what can we say?
Are they the elements we use to pave our way?
Most all parents teach their children to tell the truth.
Otherwise, we would be considered quite uncouth.

You are not born with these two elements in you.
Therefore, as we grow, we should be taught what is true.
Practicing a life of Truth and Reality,
Gives us a life of peace and practicality.

In the Bible, Truth many times is emphasized.
But Satan, with his lies, the Truth has compromised.
And those who compromise Truth have a loose living,
With deceit and no truthful life delivering.

Not just that, but their living leads direct to death.
So, regeneration is required for new breath.
Yes indeed, a "new lease on life" is what we need.
It is like planting a garden, using new seed.

We all need a new perspective to clearly see
What it means to put on the one New Man to be.
For to live in Satan's deceit leads us to death,
But life in Christ's Reality gives us new breath!

Therefore, rise-up; live in Truth and Reality,
Not just in words, but in all practicality.
For soon we will see the Judge, who reviews our deeds.
And He will review the growth of those planted seeds.

As such, we are reviewed for a crown of glory,
But that depends on our lifetime living story.

We should pray each day that we would gain more of Him,
To join other saints in the New Jerusalem!

Oh Lord, please cover us as we seek You each day.
Transform and conform us, in the God-Ordained Way.
Make us Your testament, who seek You earnestly
And give us a place with You for eternity!

TO BE OR NOT TO BE?
(Dedicated to all of us)

Yes, that is the question, "To be or not to be?"
Is this asked through strength or is it debility?
This famous line came from the dramatist, Shakespeare.
Did he question existence in valor or fear?

As many do today, he searched for a reason,
Yes, any reason that would be best in season.
What is causing man to question his being?
Why not enjoy life, instead of bedeviling?

As we go through life, each day in our existence,
We just take it for granted, with no resistance.
Some live a difficult life and some live a dream.
Regardless which one, they are all in the world stream.

But there is a better answer to the question
And I submit it to you as a suggestion.
If you believe God, you believe His creation
And that gives solution to this situation.

Yes, I know there are those who are non-believers.
And there are those with theories who are deceivers.
How can one believe that we exist by accident,
With "Big Bang" theory giving us embodiment?

There is the question of not only how, but why,
We exist and our existence to justify?
The answer is higher than the Eiffel Tower;
For it comes from God, who is the highest power!

"To be or not to be?" should not be the question,
Much more needed is, "how to be;" my suggestion.
So if you believe God created us to pray,
Then, you can enjoy your life the God-ordained way!

As such, forget about "To be or not to be?"
Today you have your existence, as you can see.
So give thanks to the One who made it possible,
Which is the only scenario plausible!

A WISE-PEOPLE PROVERB
(Dedicated to all mankind)

The wisest of all people build-up their own home,
But the stupid ones tear it down, from bad seeds sown.
This comes from poor practices, not keeping God's word.
Yes, we need to follow His words that we have heard.

Search for wisdom and be not a wisdom mocker.
Be full of wisdom, to be a household anchor.
Therefore, search for wisdom and stay away from fools.
For they give knowledge they have
learned from deviant schools.

Wisdom of sensible ones guides their way of life.
It gives them a better life and helps avoid some strife.
Because fools reject good advice and deny guilt,
They cannot have a good home life that is well-built.

Be not gullible, believing just anything.
Be sensible; watch your step and joyfully sing.
That way, you can be happy with a joyful heart.
Then, with a happy home, you know you did your part.

So, know that whoever controls his mouth, lives clean
And he who listens well, much wisdom will he glean.

Therefore, be not slothful, but indomitable,
Seeking more wisdom, for a household miracle!

Good sons and daughters listen to father's discipline.
Starting in this way is how children should begin.
It is the beginning of righteousness, with grace,
Helping us stay out of trouble, in God's embrace.

Just remember that lazy hunters get no prey
And they do have a tendency to go astray.
So, seek wisdom and righteousness for a good life
And you will be good with God and free from most strife!

THE BRIDGE OF TIME
(Dedicated to all who would listen)

Something very old is here,
But hard to identify.
It is not for us to fear,
But, it we should verify.

Older than the oldest one,
At the beginning of time,
When the light came from the sun,
And the sun began to shine.

Out from eternity past,
There came something we call time.
It would run, not slow nor fast,
But steady in a straight line.

So, wherever you may go,
Whatever you may choose,
There is something you should know.
You gain age, but time you lose.

As such, you may wish to think,
About where you stand right now.
Have a plan; stand on the brink,
To finish the race somehow.

And that is how it should be,
For us on the Bridge of Time.
However, some cannot see
The best way for them to shine.

So, take heed that you should know,
Spiritually how to shine,
How to love, work, walk and grow,
As you cross the Bridge of Time!

WHAT ABOUT THE BRIDGE OF TIME?

I have often thought of a commonality,
Which is for all mankind a true reality.
However, as it is a case of common kind,
Unimportant to most, or put it out of mind.

That is, the concept of time in our daily life,
Which is common to all for pleasure or for strife.
We tend to rush through life, caring for chosen chores.
Then, we wonder why time passed so fast in our course.

Good advice is given, right under our noses;
Do not be in a rush, "Pause and smell the roses."
The Bridge of Time always did give us "mañana,"
But do not expect only heavenly mana.

Wise men plan according to an age decision.
But to plan in the age requires a clear vision.
Solomon said, "Nothing is new under the sun."
Learning God/man history; wisdom has begun!

And so it is on the Bridge of Time for us all.
We need to be alert to the age and its call,
So that the response we give will be the right one
And we will discover something "old" under the sun.

Each old discovery is a vision quite true,
Revealed to us in our age, that we never knew.
As such, true wisdom dictates new discoveries
Of old truths that give us living realities.

Yes, new inventions give interest to most of us,
But most of them are replaced, like the abacus.
So it behooves us to discover a true vision,
That will give us a righteous living decision!

THE TIME THAT MADE ME, ME

Long ago and far away, in a land that time forgot,
Before the days of Dylan or the dawn of Camelot;
There lived a race of innocents and they were you and me.
And this took place long ago, in the
Time That Made Me, Me.

For Ike was in the White House, in
that land where we were born;
Where navels were for oranges and Peyton Place was porn.
We learned to gut a muffler; and we liked being free;
And we liked that freedom, in the
Time That Made Me, Me.

We longed for love and romance, and waited for our Prince,
And Eddie Fisher married Liz, and no one's seem him since.

We danced to 'Little Darlin' and sang to 'Stagger Lee;'
We cried for Buddy Holly, in the Time That Made Me, Me.

Only girls wore earrings then and 3 was one too many;
And only boys wore flat-top cuts,
except for Jean McKinney.
And only in our wildest dreams did we expect to see,
A boy named George with lipstick, in
the Time That Made Me, Me.

We fell for Frankie Avalon; Annette was oh, so nice,
And when they made a movie, they never made it twice.
We didn't have a Star Trek five, or psycho Two and Three;
Or Rocky-Rambo, plenty, in the Time That Made Me, Me.

Miss Kitty had a heart of gold and Chester had a limp,
And Reagan was a Democrat, whose co-star was a chimp.
We had a Mister Wizard, but not a Mister T;
Oprah couldn't talk yet, in the Time That Made Me, Me.

We had our share of heroes; we never thought they'd go;
At least, not Bobby Darin or Marilyn Monroe.
For youth was still eternal and life was yet to be;
Thought Elvis was forever, in the Time That Made Me, Me.

We'd never seen the rock band that was grateful to be Dead,
And Airplanes weren't named Jefferson
and Zeppelins were not lead.

And Beatles lived in gardens then
and Monkees lived in trees;
Madonna was a virgin, in the Time That Made Me Me.

We'd never heard of microwaves, or telephones in cars,
And babies might be bottle-fed, but
they weren't grown in jars.
And pumping iron got wrinkles out
and "gay' meant fancy-free,
And dorms were never coed, in the
Time That Made Me, Me.

We had not seen enough of jets to talk about the lag,
And microchips were what (remained),
at the bottom of the bag.
And hardware was a box of nails and
bytes came from a flea,
And rocket ships were fiction, in the
Time That Made Me, Me.

Buicks came with portholes and side
shows came with freaks,
And bathing suits came big enough
to cover both your cheeks.
And Coke came just in bottles and skirts below the knee,
And Castro came to power, near the
Time That Made Me, Me.

We had no Crest with Fluoride; we had no Hill Street Blues,
And neither had we any doubts, of which restroom to use.
We had no patterned pantyhose, or Lipton herbal tea;
Or prime-time ad for condoms, in the
Time That Made Me, Me.

There were no Golden arches, no Perrier to chill,
And fish were not called Wanda and
cats were not called Bill.
And middle-age was 35 and old was forty-three,
And ancient were our parents, in the
Time That Made Me, Me.

But all things have a season, or so we've heard them say,
And now instead of Maybelline, we swear by Retin-A.
They send us invitations to join the AARP,
Yes, we came a long way, from the
Time That Made Me, Me.

So now we face a brave new world, in slightly larger jeans,
And wonder why they use small print in all the magazines.
And we tell our children's children of the way it used to be;
Long ago and far away, in that Time That Made Me, Me.

POST SCRIPT

In closing this, my third published book, I simply wish to give readers a happy "Adiós." I hope that you have perceived the differential comparison of the last poem to the others. I also hope you enjoyed and learned a little something from my many years of traveling and many varied experiences around the USA and other parts of this world. It is obvious that I have a preference for Hispanic oriented countries, due to the fact that my lovely wife is from Durango, Mexico and I am fluent in the Spanish language (read, write & speak), as are also my two younger children, who are now grown and educated.

Now, before we finish, I would like to say something about the term, "change," which is a very important factor in all our lives. It needs to be viewed and addressed here to augment what has been presented about "Firm, Fair and Consistent." Changing situations in our lives, mostly in our younger years, is a fairly constant factor we have had to deal with, sometimes just occasionally and sometimes frequently. It depends on our age, our environment and activities. By now, I would say that after reading this far, you would agree that learning to apply the FFC process in changing situations can significantly help for some type of successful accommodation and even adaptation to any new situation. So as to emphasize this point, I am giving a long quotation by a newspaper writer, Bill Modisette. It is from the Odessa American newspaper dated, 02 Feb 2017. I give it to you for the reason that I could not say it any better.

"I have had to endure a number of unwanted changes in my almost 50 years in the newspaper industry, but I also must concede that if the changes were not forced on us there would be very little progress in the world. Most individuals would likely never make a change in the way they did their work if somebody else did not insist on it. Of course, the person who can adapt and embrace the change at least to some degree, is usually better off. A good type example of one man who grew-up in the world of cowboys, but who was able to make the transition to modern society, was Bob Beverly, who worked on various ranches in Texas, New Mexico and Oklahoma, during the final years of the 19th century and later served as sheriff of Midland County (Texas) and as a lawman in New Mexico in the early 20th century."

This is one example of someone applying the virtues in his characteristics, of "Firm, Fair and Consistent," for a significant change in his life, so he could adapt to the changing times and the need for a change in his own personal situation. Of course, that is an example of a situation that is likely a bit more drastic than what we may usually face in our more modern and convenient times. But nevertheless, when we are faced with some necessary changes, whether they are temporary or permanent, it is evident that we need to have the necessary personal character to do it and adapt appropriately to the situation. Now, there is one other thing that I definitely feel obligated to do and wish to say. First, I wish to acknowledge the help of my daughter Ana, for the help in reviewing this book and editing it. Then, I will also speak of my younger brother, Terry, who urged the writing of this book.

I wish to acknowledge the strong encouragement of my younger brother, Terry, who "pressed" urgently for me to write this book. He was so impressed by the terms I used in counseling of youth and others, "Firm, Fair and Consistent," that he urged me to write this book, with those terms being the central point of content for the book. Furthermore, he strongly gave me impetus to write my first book, which I wrote and published, "One Bad Night In Mexico." He said it was a very important event in my life, as a "near-death" experience, in Durango, Mexico with my father-in-law. His last strong argument was that my two children were very young in that time period and that I should write the book and document what actually happened back in 1988. It would be that, when they grew-up, they could read about what really happened and not just hear a "tall tale" about it.

However, I did write my second book with my own internal motivation, "The Practical Poet," which is a book of 150 of my poems written in the years from 1967 to 2015. Maybe the internal motivational factor was just because, for me, writing poetry is my most enjoyable writing. And I think you will be able to see that for a fact, because there is quite a variety of subjects, themes and styles in this collection of poems and I am sure that you will be able to find a few of them to peak your interest. Yes, I know that my poetry style will appear a bit different from most traditional poetry, but the content is what is most important.

As you can see by my statement, I needed a "motivational push" to get me moving to write the first and third books. We all need some motivational impetus in our lives to move us toward a goal or to do some kind of deed. But then, we need FFC to carry us through it successfully. As such I hope all you readers do get at least a little of something, or even more than a little, worthwhile from my writings and I wish that God would bless you all, but especially those believers in Him.

I just would say one other thing, before I close this book. It appears that the great majority of us in this world seek to have some form of "success," in whatever it is that interests us. And whatever that may be is probably supposed to give us a bit of happiness, pleasure or satisfaction. However, when the end of our life here on Earth arrives and all is "said and done," there is always the final question: "What awaits me, 'on the other side'?" As such, that is the reason that much emphasis is placed on the spiritual aspects of our lives in this book. That is the reason I will tell you that, regardless of all the worldly accomplishments that one may attain in this lifetime, it is what God counts as important, which is truly gainful and profitable for us with Him, as He judges us, for determining what lies ahead for us "on the other side!" May the Good Lord have mercy on all of us and supply us with His grace, that we may see and understand this basic principle of life and adjust our living accordingly!! And may He bless all who read and apply His words of LIFE.

TS Bola

Author

ABOUT THE AUTHOR

Author was born in 1937, living most of his life in a small Texas town and having most of his education including high school.

While growing up, author enjoyed very much the sport of football and played it many years. As a matter of fact, that was the main reason he wanted to attend high school and not for the academics. As such, he just barely graduated from high school, mainly because all he wanted to do was to play football. He made enough passing grades so he would be eligible to play football. However, his practice was not all in vain, because he had a good enough team in 1953 to win the Class A, Texas State Championship. Thank God, he was so dedicated to football; not that he was a great talent, but because it required a certain discipline.

Printed in the United States
By Bookmasters